W9-CBR-949

Gargoyles, Girders & Glass Houses

MAGNIFICENT MASTER BUILDERS

by Bo Zaunders

illustrated by Roxie Munro

WITHDRAWN

Dutton Children's Books · New York

To my father, Erik

—B.Z.

To my nephew Andrew Carr Wood

—R.M.

Text copyright © 2004 by Bo Zaunders
Illustrations copyright © 2004 by Roxie Munro
All rights reserved.

Library of Congress Cataloging-in-Publication Data

Zaunders, Bo.
Gargoyles, girders & glass houses/by Bo Zaunders; illustrated by Roxie Munro.
—1st ed.
v. cm.
Includes bibliographical references (p. x).
Contents: Pippo's Dome—Mosques of Sinan—Lisboa "The Little Cripple"—The Roeblings and the Brooklyn Bridge—Gustave Eiffel—Gaudí—Van Alen and the Chrysler Building.
ISBN 0-525-47284-3
1. Architects—Biography—Juvenile literature. 2. Architecture, Modern—Juvenile literature. [1. Architects. 2. Architecture.] I. Title: Gargoyles, girders, and glass houses. II. Munro, Roxie, ill. III. Title.
NA500.Z38 2004
720'.9—dc22   2003028192

Published in the United States by Dutton Children's Books,
a division of Penguin Young Readers Group
345 Hudson Street, New York, New York 10014
www.penguin.com

Designed by Gloria Cheng
Manufactured in China
First Edition
10 9 8 7 6 5 4 3 2 1

j 720.9
ZAU

Contents

Introduction

Imagine wrapping yourself up in warm, soft furs and falling asleep on a bed of ice. You wake up in a hotel where everything, including a restaurant and a wedding chapel, is made of crystal clear ice and snow. In Lapland, Sweden, there is such a hotel. In spring it melts, and each winter it has to be built up again. Most buildings are less extreme and, fortunately, more durable.

The great pyramids of Egypt, built to hold the remains of kings who died some 4,500 years ago, are still standing. Another burial place that has stood the test of time is the Taj Mahal. Commissioned by a distraught seventeenth-century Indian emperor after his wife died, it was built in her memory and is now the world's most glorious tomb.

Architecture is enormously varied, ranging from the ordinary and ugly to the exceptional and beautiful. It has the ability to inspire our imaginations and excite curiosity in many ways, yet it is so much a part of everyday life that we tend to take it for granted.

Shelter is the primary reason for architecture, but there are others. Fortresses are built for defense; factories and offices are workplaces; a bridge is for transport, a stadium hosts sports, and some of the most remarkable and beautiful structures ever built are places of worship. This is particularly true of the Middle Ages in Europe, with its many grand cathedrals.

Behind the great structures of the world lie the toil of millions of ordinary workers, whose labor, frequently fraught with danger, has often been overlooked. According to the Greek historian Herodotus, it took twenty to thirty years for 100,000 men to build the Cheops pyramid. In Europe during the Middle Ages, centuries often passed before the completion of a single cathedral.

Not only are the workers unknown—most of the chief builders from long ago are also lost to history, including those who erected the great European cathedrals. It wasn't until the Renaissance in the fifteenth century that architects became prized as artists and individuals—which brings us to Filippo Brunelleschi, the Italian genius who, unlike the builders of the Middle Ages, was far from anonymous. His story begins this book.

As we planned *Gargoyles, Girders & Glass Houses*, Roxie and I found ourselves facing some difficult choices. There are dozens of fascinating builders we might have included. The English architect Christopher Wren was one of them. After the Great Fire of 1666, he practically rebuilt the entire city of London—and designed St. Paul's Cathedral. (We once visited this magnificent church, the third largest in the world. Roxie and I carried on a conversation in the Whispering Gallery. Standing at opposite sides of the great dome, we spoke quietly into the wall and could clearly hear one another from 112 feet away!)

We also considered Charles Garnier, who built the Paris Opera House. It is Paris's most distinguished theater, featuring not only a magnificent nineteenth-century facade and foyer but an enormous behind-the-scenes apparatus large enough to accommodate any production, including live horses running on a rotating stage. Most fascinating may be what's beneath the opera, underground and hidden from sight: a labyrinth of dark corridors and a subterranean river—the fabled domain of the Phantom of the Opera.

Frank Lloyd Wright, Julia Morgan, Maya Lin, and Frank Gehry are other builders we thought about. I was particularly intrigued by Gehry, one of today's leading architects, a Californian famous for his playfulness. Among his many creations are the two joined buildings in Prague, nick-named "Fred and Ginger"—because they look as if they are dancing with each other, like the famous movie stars Fred Astaire and Ginger Rogers.

Another Gehry design is the new Guggenheim Museum in Bilbao, Spain. Affectionately referred to as *La Alcachofa,* "the Artichoke," it is sheathed in titanium, a material normally used for building aircraft. Its metallic walls twist and gyrate and, at one juncture, slide under a bridge.

Glass is another unusual building material. An example is Philip Johnson's Glass House in Connecticut, in which the furniture appears suspended in thin air, blending with the surrounding woods. There's also the entrance to the Louvre in Paris. Chinese-born American architect I. M. Pei created a stir when—availing himself of a shape rarely used in architecture since the days of the pharaohs—he added a glass pyramid to the venerable old museum.

Pei, incidentally, once drew inspiration for a design from an experience he had at age eleven, when his mother brought him to a serene mountain retreat in China. "Listen to the silence," she said as she made him kneel down and meditate. The kneeling position became quite painful, but Pei persevered. For hours he sat in total silence, hearing absolutely nothing. Then, from the bamboo shoot next to him came a faint snapping sound, followed by another—the sound of a bamboo tree sprouting new growth. Pei never forgot it. After finishing the Louvre pyramid, he built the Bank of China, one of Hong Kong's most famous skyscrapers, in which each floor pushes up out of the one below—like growth rings in a bamboo tree.

Pei's use of a childhood experience should not be surprising. The vision and passion of a true artist—be it a painter or an architect—will often draw on early memories for inspiration.

So why didn't we include him and some of the others? Partly

because there's only so much space in a forty-eight-page book and partly because we became more and more intrigued with the special stories and challenges behind the work of the engineers and architects we *did* pick. Our research was wonderful fun and introduced us to fascinating builders and building projects from around the world.

We wanted to touch upon as many centuries and countries as possible. After exploring the Renaissance in Florence, Italy, we turn to Turkey for a chapter on Sinan, the master of sixteenth-century Ottoman architecture. Then there's Brazil's Lisboa, who, despite a crippling disease, built some of the most beautiful churches of the colonial era. In the 1800s, we have German-born John Roebling and his son Washington erecting the Brooklyn Bridge, and another great engineer, the Frenchman Gustave Eiffel. The twentieth century is represented by Antoni Gaudí in Barcelona, Spain, and Van Alen, the American who built the Chrysler Building.

In 1642, a lover of architecture wrote that "well-building hath three conditions: Commoditie, Firmness, and Delight." By that he meant that architecture has not one but three distinct purposes: it must shelter human activity (commoditie), be built to last (firmness), and be an object of beauty (delight).

From Brunelleschi to Van Alen, these builders certainly knew how to use their skills to create practical shelters. Each also had a special talent for building works that never fail to delight us.

PIPPO'S DOME

Through the large opening up above shimmered the blue Tuscan sky. But down on the floor, with dozens of men working, the air was dusty and the noise deafening. In the center of it all stood the wonder of the day—a giant hoist.

Powered by two oxen, it creaked and rattled as it raised marble, brick, stone, and mortar to the work site above. Much like a modern bicycle, the hoist used different gears. One gear reversed so that the animals below didn't have to turn around to bring the rope down.

It was the spring of 1422. In Florence, Italy, the construction of a dome for the cathedral of Santa Maria del Fiore was finally underway. In charge of it was Filippo Brunelleschi, a short, bald, middle-aged man, with a hooked nose, dirty clothes, and a suspicious, even belligerent, look about him. To get started on the most magnificent dome in the world, Brunelleschi needed such a hoist, so he had no choice but to invent one.

The cathedral of Santa Maria del Fiore was the city's most ambitious building project. In 1296, the commune of Florence decided to replace an ancient and dilapidated church. What we want, the commune declared, is "a more beautiful and honorable temple than in any part of Tuscany." Entire forests were cut down to provide the timber. Flotillas of boats brought huge slabs of marble from along the Arno River. The foundation was laid, and for the next hundred years, work progressed steadily.

There was one problem, however. The 30-foot scale model of the cathedral, which stood on the work site, included an enormous octagonal dome, which would rise to 300 feet—the height of a thirty-story building—and have a diameter of 130 feet. At the time the model was made, no one in Florence—or anywhere else—knew how to construct such a dome. The builders believed that when the time came to build the dome, architects with more advanced knowledge would, with the help of God, manage to do it. Yet, a hundred years later, the unbuilt dome of Santa Maria del Fiore was still the architectural puzzle of the age.

Finally, in 1418, the Opera del Duomo—the Wool Merchants of Florence, now in charge of the cathedral—announced a competition. Over a dozen proposals were submitted. Expecting a mason or a carpenter to solve the puzzle, the merchants were surprised to find that the most promising model was conceived by a goldsmith and clockmaker named Filippo Brunelleschi.

Filippo Brunelleschi—or "Pippo," as he was known to everyone—was forty-one years old when he won the competition. A native of Florence, he had grown up just a short walk from the cathedral work site. His father, a prosperous man, had wanted his son to become a civil servant like himself, but Pippo was not interested. Noticing the boy's practical bent and uncanny talent for solving mechanical problems, his father eventually gave in to Pippo's wishes and had him apprenticed, at age fifteen, to the workshop of a goldsmith. At this time, goldsmiths were highly regarded and not limited to working with jewelry. The most prestigious of artisans, they melted and cast all kinds of metals, decorated manuscripts with gold leaf, and designed elaborate tombs and shrines.

At twenty-one Pippo graduated as a master goldsmith. Three years later he rose to local fame by participating in a design competition, which came about because of repeated outbreaks of the Black Plague. To appease God and prevent yet another outbreak, the Guild of Cloth Merchants sponsored a competition for a new set of bronze doors for one of the city's most venerated buildings, the Baptistery of San Giovanni. Each contestant was given four sheets of bronze and ordered to execute a scene from the Old Testament: Abraham's sacrifice of his son Isaac. Of the original seven competitors, only two were deemed worthy of the prize: Pippo and another goldsmith named Lorenzo Ghiberti. When Ghiberti was finally chosen as the winner, Pippo left Florence in a huff, seeking a new life in Rome.

In Pippo's day, Rome was a much diminished city from the time of the proud Roman Empire. Endless wars, plagues, earthquakes, and epidemics had shrunk the population from one million to 25,000. Little is known about Pippo's years in Rome, except that he was seen digging around in the rubble of ancient ruins, often with his younger friend, the sculptor Donatello. Romans viewed them with suspicion, thinking they were treasure hunters looking for gold or silver. What the two young men were searching for was neither gold nor silver—it was the great art and architecture of ancient Rome, much of which had been buried and forgotten for well over a thousand years.

Still standing, however, was the Pantheon, with the world's largest dome, spanning 142 feet, and rising to a height of 143 feet. Pippo wanted to figure out how the Romans had managed to build it.

The model Pippo presented to the Florentine judges after he returned from Rome did not call for a traditional wooden framework or interior scaffolding. To give the dome stabililty, he instead proposed building it with a thick inner shell and—for protection against the weather—a thinner outer one. Also, to avoid the need for external buttresses, and for extra strength, he proposed to weave some of the building bricks into an interlocking herringbone pattern and add girdles of wooden chains, reinforced with iron cramps. Exactly how all this was to be achieved he did not make clear, stating that it would have to be a process of trial and error.

In 1423, following the construction of the hoist, work on the dome was in full swing. Every morning, masons and other laborers climbed to a work site that rose higher and higher, with walls that leaned inward at an ever more alarming angle. To give his workers a sense of security and prevent dizziness, Pippo installed a narrow platform, projecting from the masonry, and as a safety measure he gave some of the masons leather harnesses. Working until sunset, they all brought lunch with them, and eventually a little kitchen was installed between the two shells. Work progressed steadily, year after year. Huge quantities of white marble had to be shipped and added to the ribs that defined the eight corners of the dome. Sometimes, because of bad weather, operations were halted. The inventive Pippo met each new challenge straight on. When the hoist proved insufficient, he promptly constructed a crane for more precise delivery of building material. Poised hundreds of feet above the cathedral's stone floor, it had a small platform at the top for the operator—surely one of the most giddying and dangerous workplaces imaginable. Remarkably, in the thirteen long years it took to finish the dome, there were only two casualties.

In 1436, the dome finally stood ready. It rose to 300 feet above the ground—without the lantern on the top, which was added ten years later.

Exactly how Brunelleschi worked out all the details in the construction of his famous dome is still a matter of debate. Always suspicious and afraid that people might steal his ideas, he kept few records; much of what he wrote down was in a secret code. But he became the most renowned architect of his day. Even Michelangelo, who a hundred years later built St. Peter's dome in Rome, conceded that he would never be able to surpass Pippo. The old Florentine dream of an "enormous construction towering above the heavens, vast enough to cover the entire Tuscan population with its shadow" had come true at last.

THE MOSQUES OF SINAN

In 1555, the Ottoman Empire in Turkey was at the peak of its power, and Sinan, the empire's most illustrious architect, was starting yet another project. He had built palaces, harems, tombs, schools, poorhouses, aqueducts, and hospitals. More than anything, he was the undisputed master builder of some eighty great mosques—places of worship, where Muslims pray.

But the mosque he built on the sixth hill of the old city of Istanbul was different. It was for Princess Mihrimah, the sultan's daughter, with whom he was secretly in love. Because she was a married woman, tied to a man she didn't love, Sinan could never speak of his affection. Only through the mosque would he be able to show his true feelings. "Let me feel as free in my mosque as if it were out of doors," the princess had said. So he set about to create his most radiant structure. As a princess, Mihrimah was entitled to two minarets (towers), but Sinan decided to erect only one—to express the sad loneliness of her life.

14

age ninety-nine. The Ottoman Empire was created in 1453, when Istanbul—then called Constantinople—fell into the hands of the Turks. Replacing the thousand-year Roman Empire, it lasted until 1923 and made its greatest mark in the history of art and architecture in the fifteen hundreds, in the period of Sinan.

During the last five decades of his life, Sinan was busy indeed. A list of his achievements includes 133 mosques, 67 schools, 34 palaces, 33 public baths, 22 mausoleums, 3 hospitals, 16 almshouses, 7 madrassas, and 12 caravansaries. When he was eighty, Sinan, having reached the pinnacle of his artistic career, designed the Selimiye Mosque in Edirne, Turkey, near the Bulgarian border. Built for Süleyman's son and successor, Selim II, it is a vast, towering structure filled with light that illuminates walls decorated with rich geometric designs, arabesques, and phrases from the holy book of Islam, the Koran. Many, including Sinan himself, considered it his best work.

Even though it was said that the young princess Mihrimah was Sinan's great love, it would be more accurate to say that she was his inspiration, his muse. His real, lifelong love affair was with architecture.

O Aleijadinho
"The Little Cripple"

As always, he arrived at daybreak before there were any people around to gape in horror at his disfigurement. Januarío lifted him off his mule. Mauricío adjusted his leather knee pads and strapped a chisel and a mallet to his crippled hands. Agostinho, meanwhile, tools in hand, stood ready to help. These men were his three slaves, always with him.

Next he climbed the high stepladder, something he could still do despite the loss of practically all his toes. The unfinished statue of the prophet Jonah confronted him. Before setting to work, afraid that people might see his face and shrink away with fear and loathing, he covered himself with a hooded cloak. Work was slow and painful, and lasted all day. Not until nightfall, under the cover of darkness, was he willing to have his servants bring him back home.

He was Antônio Francisco Lisboa, better known as O Aleijadinho, "The Little Cripple," in the 1700s, Brazil's most celebrated sculptor and architect.

In 1698, gold was discovered in the mountainous state of Minas Gerais, a wild uninhabited land about two hundred miles north of Rio de Janeiro in Brazil. Immediately, thousands of fortune seekers poured into the region. They found plenty of gold, and as towns rose quickly, Minas Gerais prospered.

One who benefited from the building boom was Manuel Lisboa, a Portuguese carpenter, who in 1720 settled in Ouro Prêto, one of the fastest-growing new towns. From carpentry, Manuel worked his way up, designing and erecting mansions, public buildings, and churches, gaining prominence as a major contractor and architect.

In 1738, a son was born to him and one of his black African slaves. Because his mother was a slave, the boy was considered one, too. But Manuel freed him at baptism—at which time the boy was given the name Antônio Francisco Lisboa.

Antônio grew up a robust child, full of curiosity and with a great zest for life. Like many children at that time, he received no formal schooling but somehow learned to read and write. He also took lessons in drawing and sculpting and, from working under his father's supervision, acquired a knowledge of architecture. For years, father and son worked together. Then, having learned everything his father could teach him, Antônio started out on his own, an architect and sculptor.

In the 1600s, a new architectural style had developed in Europe and spread throughout the western world. Called Baroque, it was ideal for an architect who was also a sculptor. It was highly ornamental and called for richly decorated facades, doorways, and interiors.

Although Antônio built bridges and mansions, and designed public fountains, his favorite projects were churches, which he decorated lavishly. Embellishing them with sculptures of angels, saints, and mythological beings, Antônio used soapstone, a mineral indigenous to the Minas Gerais region. Soft, with a soapy feel and slightly grayish color, it substituted for European marble and became part of a distinct style Antônio developed on his own, and which is now known as Barroco Mineiro. A much admired example of it is the Saint Francis of Assisi Church in Ouro Prêto, which he built in the 1760s.

In 1777, when Antônio was thirty-nine years old and at the height of his career, he was struck by leprosy or some unknown disease. Gradually, it deformed his body. His face became horribly disfigured; swollen eyelids obstructed his vision; his fingers and toes became paralyzed and started to fall off. But, despite intense agony, Antônio refused to give up. As an artist, he instead became freer and even more dedicated, though increasingly dependent on the help of his three slaves.

However, from being a joyful person, Antônio turned bitter and anguished. His awareness of what people might think when they saw his face made him immediately suspicious, and he would sometimes lash out in rage at those praising his work, assuming that they were actually mocking him. Now he saw the world as cruel; yet to those close to him whom he trusted, he remained cheerful and jovial.

The statue of the Prophet Jonah was part of a large project: sandstone depictions of the Twelve Prophets symmetrically arranged on the steps and terraces leading to the Sanctuary of Bom Jesus de Matozinhos in Congonhas do Campo. The assignment also included sixty-six life-size figures in cedarwood, portraying scenes from the Bible and placed in six different chapels. Many consider the statues of Congonhas do Campo to be Antônio's most expressive and beautiful work.

Loved by all Brazilians, he is still affectionately called O Aleijadinho, "The Little Cripple."

THE BROOKLYN BRIDGE AND THE ROEBLINGS

He was sitting on a tiny swing attached to a single cable that stretched across the East River. Hundreds of boats thronged in the water below; spectators by the thousands lined the shore. Every eye was glued on this one man.

Finally, after years of work and serious setbacks, it looked like some real progress was being made. First the enormous wooden boxes the newspapers called caissons had been sunk into the river. Then came the towers, rising and rising, until they completely dominated the New York skyline. But to support the roadway not yet built, steel cables were needed, the first of which had now been spun.

To celebrate the event, waving his hat as the people below cheered wildly, master mechanic Frank Farrington let himself go, gliding the entire length from one shore to the other.

He was the first person to make it across the Brooklyn Bridge.

23

Farrington's crossing—which was greeted with the ringing of church bells and the screaming of factory whistles—took place on August 25, 1876. Construction was then into its sixth year, and seven more would pass before the Brooklyn Bridge, the greatest engineering feat of the nineteenth century, was completed.

For decades, the people of New York had talked about a bridge that would join Brooklyn and the island of Manhattan. The problem was the East River. Nearly half a mile wide and swirling with strong currents, it was one of the busiest stretches of water in the world, plied by a steady stream of ferries, steamers, and clipper ships. "If there is to be a bridge," commented one newspaperman, "it must take one grand flying leap from shore to shore over the masts of the ships. There must be only one great arch all the way across. Surely this must be a wonderful bridge."

No bridge of such magnitude had ever been built, and only one man stepped forward with a proposal for how to do it. He was John Roebling, a German engineer and immigrant.

The first time it occurred to John Roebling, a prominent bridge builder and manufacturer of steel wires, that he might be the man for the job—or so the story goes—was one cold morning in 1853. He and his sixteen-year-old son, Washington, were taking the ferry to Brooklyn and got stuck for hours in the icebound East River. Roebling, a man of little patience, became increasingly irritable. But as a result, standing on deck next to his son, he "then and there saw a bridge in his mind's eye."

Fourteen years later, in 1867, he presented his plan to city officials and investors. It called for two identical massive towers, 268 feet high. Each tower would feature two pointed arches, a hundred feet tall, that would look like "majestic cathedral windows or triumphal gateways." Not only would this be the greatest bridge in existence, Roebling stated, it would also be a great work of art. With him at the presentation was Washington, now an engineer like his father, and knowledgeable about the project.

In 1869, as the plan was approved and work was set to begin, John Roebling met with a tragic accident. Standing on a Brooklyn pier, absorbed with his own thoughts, he didn't notice an approaching ferry. Washington shouted a warning, but before his father could move to safety, the ferry slammed into the pier and crushed his foot. John Roebling died from an infection a month later.

His death was a blow to everyone, especially Washington. His beloved father was gone. What would happen to the bridge? Because Washington was the only one intimately involved with the plans for its construction, the sponsors of the bridge asked him to take over as chief engineer. "Here I was at the age of thirty-two," Washington later said, "suddenly in charge of the most stupendous engineering project of the age!" It was a daunting challenge. In time, he would have nearly a thousand men under his command.

First he had to build the two towers. If they were erected on the soft, muddy river bottom, the bridge would be unstable, so to lay a firm foundation, Washington built two caissons, one for each tower. Caissons (after the French word *caisson,* meaning "chest") had previously been constructed in Europe, but none of a size comparable to what Washington needed. Almost as big as a city block, the first caisson, on the Brooklyn side, was a gigantic wooden box with a thick roof, strong sides, and an underwater chamber with no floor. After the

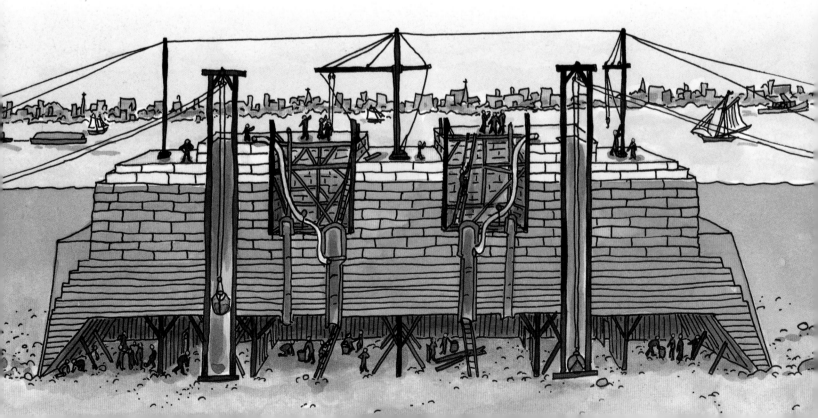

caisson had been launched and settled on the riverbed, the chamber was drained of water and filled with compressed air. Workmen entered through special air locks. Working in shifts, nearly a hundred at a time, they shoveled out mud and rocks, disposed of through ingeniously designed water shafts. As the caisson lowered, it would eventually reach bedrock. It was grueling work, lasting for months, and fraught with unexpected dangers.

Digging was well underway when, one evening, a fire started inside the thick wooden roof of the caisson. Washington rushed to the underwater site. All night he helped his men try to extinguish the fire which, fanned by the high-pressure air, kept spreading. Finally Washington had no choice but to let the water in and flood the caisson. Work was halted for three weeks. Even worse, after emerging from his extended stay below water, Washington collapsed, struck by what would become known as caisson disease, or the bends.

In the 1800s, little was understood of this sickness, which occurs when someone deep underwater surfaces too quickly. It can cause severe cramps, paralysis, even death. Washington was so badly stricken that he spent the next few years in a wheelchair in his Brooklyn apartment. From there, with field glasses to view the work site, he continued with his duties as chief engineer, aided by his capable wife, Emily.

Though not an engineer, Emily became Washington's only contact with the outside world, delivering his instructions to engineers and foremen. At the time, it was unheard of for a woman to work on a construction project, but the even-tempered and intelligent Emily soon gained the respect of everyone. Without her, Washington might have been unable to complete the bridge.

The tower on the Brooklyn side was erected from a depth of 45 feet below sea level. The caisson for the Manhattan-side tower needed much more digging. As the workers went deeper and deeper, still not finding solid rock, many were struck with caisson disease, and to Washington's horror, two died. What was he to do—jeopardize the stability of the bridge or risk his workers' lives? Fortunately, the workers soon discovered hard-packed sand and gravel beneath the caisson, ground solid enough to support the tower. The digging stopped—at a depth of 78 feet.

Everyone watched with excitement as the two towers rose. At a time when buildings rarely exceeded three stories, these mammoth structures, when completed, would reach a height of 276 feet—the equivalent of a 25-story building. Next came the two anchorages, one on each shore, to connect the towers to land and secure the cables needed to hold up the roadway.

Master mechanic Frank Harrington's crossing marked the beginning of the stringing of 3,500 miles of steel wire. After the wires had

27

been shuttled back and forth in a process called spinning, they were woven together to form four 16-inch-thick cables. This work was done from small wooden perches that hung hundreds of feet above the river, and mostly by sailors, who were used to working on the masts of tall ships.

Finally came the bridge floor, supported by some 200 smaller cables suspended down from the four main cables. On it, Washington put roads, railroad tracks, and—so that people could enjoy the fabulous view—a pedestrian walkway called the Promenade.

The bridge opened on May 24, 1883. It was a glorious spring day. Stores, businesses, even schools closed, and some 100,000 people celebrated. As music played and a procession led by the President of the United States, Chester A. Arthur, crossed the bridge from Manhattan to Brooklyn, the crowd went wild. Alone by his sickroom window in Brooklyn Heights sat Washington, watching the spectacle through his field glasses. Later that day he met with the president, who congratulated him. "Why all the fuss and ceremony?" he is reported to have said. "Why not put up a sign that says THE BRIDGE IS OPEN?"

After the opening New Yorkers fell in love with the Brooklyn Bridge. Thousands thronged the Promenade, taking in the view, marveling at the sight of seagulls flying below them. The toll for every pedestrian was one cent, a pig was two, and for every horse-drawn wagon, the charge went up to ten cents.

Hailed by some as the Eighth Wonder of the World, the bridge has loomed large in the imaginations of many writers, including poets Walt Whitman and Stephen Crane. This is what one inspired fan wrote:

> Against the city's gleaming spires,
> Above the ships that ply the stream,
> A bridge of haunting beauty stands—
> Fulfillment of an artist's dream.

EIFFEL'S TOWER

The great Paris tower was underway. From each corner of a broad base the size of a football field, four spidery iron structures rose, curving inward in one majestic sweep toward the middle. The construction—a web of connecting girders—called for 300 workers to assemble some 15,000 pieces of iron and snap 2.5 million rivets into place. This would be the world's tallest man-made structure, reaching a height of 300 meters (934 feet). A glorious demonstration of modern engineering, it was conceived by Gustave Eiffel, the most illustrious engineer of nineteenth-century France.

Eiffel planned it to be the focal point of the International Exhibition of Paris in 1889, commemorating the 100th birthday of the French Revolution.

After that, since the tower had no practical use, it was scheduled to be torn down.

30

It took two years, two months, and five days to build the Eiffel Tower. Eiffel used wrought iron (iron that is molded, or "wrought," into various designs), which was a relatively new building material at the time, used primarily for the construction of bridges and aqueducts. As the tower rose steadily, becoming by far the most prominent feature of the French capital, not everyone approved. In fact, many Parisians objected vehemently. They thought that this huge metal object was an insult to France's good taste. "Useless and monstrous," one news-paper critic called it. Another felt it looked like a "truly tragic street lamp," and a third described it as an "odious column of bolted metal."

But Eiffel was not discouraged. His was the time of the new industrial age, of factories, railroads, and steamships. "Why should we disguise the industrial nature of iron?" he replied when questioned about his choice of material.

Alexandre-Gustave Eiffel was born in 1832 in Dijon, France, the son of a coal merchant. After engineering studies in Paris, he began working for an architectural firm that specialized in railroads and bridges. He advanced quickly. At age twenty-six, he was already in charge of building an iron railway bridge in Bordeaux. At thirty-four, he started his own engineering firm, putting up bridges, viaducts, facto-ries, and railroad stations all around the world. The railroad bridge he built over the Douro River in Portugal in 1877 established him as one of the great engi-neers of his day. Unlike any previous bridge, it featured an enormous iron arch, spanning 488 feet. Eiffel married and had five children. An early photo of him shows a rather attractive prosperous-looking man with a neatly trimmed beard.

Called the Magician of Iron, Eiffel's mathematical prowess and attention to detail were legendary. He left nothing to chance. To put the tower project on paper took 18 months and 30 draftsmen working full time. Every rivet of the 2.5 million need-ed for the structure had its designated place, down to a fraction of a millimeter.

Precision was essential. All the sections of the tower—some 15,000 pieces—were prefabricated outside Paris, then brought by horse-drawn wagons to the work site, where they were fastened together.

The Eiffel Tower became the hit of the International Exhibition—nearly two million people visited the tower. Still, not everyone loved this prodigious web of steel girders. A famous author was once asked why he ate his lunch there every day, since he was known to hate the sight of it. He replied, "Because it's the only place in Paris where I can't see the damn thing."

So why wasn't the Eiffel Tower torn down? Actually it almost was. What saved it was the radio broadcasting center and, later, a weather station that Eiffel installed at the top. From his office on the highest of the tower's three platforms, Eiffel continually took steps to keep his precious creation standing.

The Eiffel Tower is now France's most famous landmark. But it isn't the only well-known national symbol Eiffel was involved with. In 1885, as a token of international friendship, France presented the United States with the statue of a 305-foot-tall lady holding a torch. As the sculptor Frédéric-Auguste Bartholdi, using copper sheets, created her outer skin, Eiffel built an iron skeleton to prevent the great lady from collapsing under her own weight.

Disassembled into 350 pieces and packed in 210 crates, she was shipped to New York City and once again put together. Originally named "Liberty Enlightening the World," she is now universally known as the Statue of Liberty.

Gustave Eiffel kept working away in his test station in the sky until he was well into his eighties. Few people know that he started the Panama Canal and was the first to think of a tunnel under the English Channel and an underground rail system in Paris. But, of course, everyone is familiar with the Eiffel Tower. "I ought to be jealous of that tower," he once said. "She is more famous than I am."

33

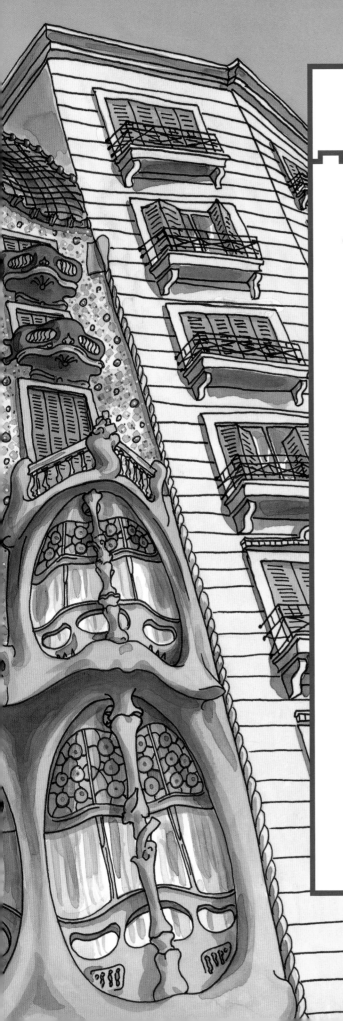

BARCELONA'S GAUDÍ

José Batlló's house in Barcelona, Spain, was beginning to look a little shabby alongside its more fashionable neighbors. So, to dress it up, Señor Batlló turned to Antoni Gaudí, the city's most inventive architect—and got a house that astonished all Barcelona.

Its walls, studded with glittering blue and green shards, billowed like the sea. Some of the windows were egg-shaped, others had balconies that resembled giant masks with bars in the openings for the eyes. The roof was even more fanciful. Eerily iridescent, the colors shifted from bluish green to golden orange. With its scalelike tiles, it reminded people of a dinosaur's backbone and was topped with a row of rounded multicolored pots and a cross that looked like some strange flower.

Because of the oval windows, some people began calling it the House of Yawns. Others, noticing slender columns that looked like shinbones, christened it the House of Bones.

35

At the time Casa Batlló was finished, in 1906, Antoni Gaudí was Spain's most controversial architect. Whether a genius or a madman, he was one of a kind. Born in 1852, the son, grandson, and great-grandson of coppersmiths, Gaudí grew up in the small town of Reus, near Barcelona, in the northeastern corner of Spain in the region known as Catalonia. As a boy he developed rheumatoid arthritis, and the soreness and pain in his joints sometimes made it difficult for him to play with other children and even to attend school. He roamed the countryside alone, making little sketches of what he saw and, generally, living in his own world of discovery and fantasy.

Gaudí felt proud of being a Catalan. His favorite books dealt with medieval history when Catalonia was a country of its own, separate from Spain. At age sixteen, Gaudí and two other boys visited the ruins of what had once been a magnificent monastery, north of his hometown. Full of enthusiasm, the boys made elaborate plans for how they might restore the place to its former glory. Because Gaudí became absorbed in every detail of the ruined monastery, his friends thought that, one day, he should eventually be the one to rebuild it. Right then and there, Gaudí decided to become an architect.

As an architectural student in Barcelona, Gaudí was well liked, although many thought him a little strange. He would occasionally skip classes so that he could spend time alone in the library, reading philosophy. Once the students were asked to draw a portal to a cemetery. Instead, Gaudí drew a hearse followed by a procession of weeping mourners. Though he failed the test, he received a top grade for his artistic brilliance.

At the beginning of his career Gaudí worked for other, more experienced architects but quickly developed a style entirely his own, drawing inspiration directly from nature, rather than from anything man-made. He was disdainful of straight lines. "They belong to men," he used to say. "Curved lines belong to God."

There are few straight lines in Gaudí's work. At Casa Batlló, a staircase with spiraling wooden handrails leads to a living room with a sculpted ceiling that joyfully swirls itself around the main light fixture. Even the pale blue walls are curved. As they arch into a ceiling, the color deepens into the deep blue of a summer's sky. Many of Gaudí's close friends were proud Catalans like himself. One, Eusebio Güell, was a successful businessman and Gaudí's most prominent patron. For him, Gaudí designed first pavilions, then a palace, and finally one of the world's quirkiest parks: the Park Güell.

Situated on a hill just outside Barcelona, the Park Güell is a kind of fairy-tale fantasy. When a visitor enters it, two mechanical gazelles, flanking the entrance, perform a little dance. A giant, tile-encrusted lizard crouches on a staircase,

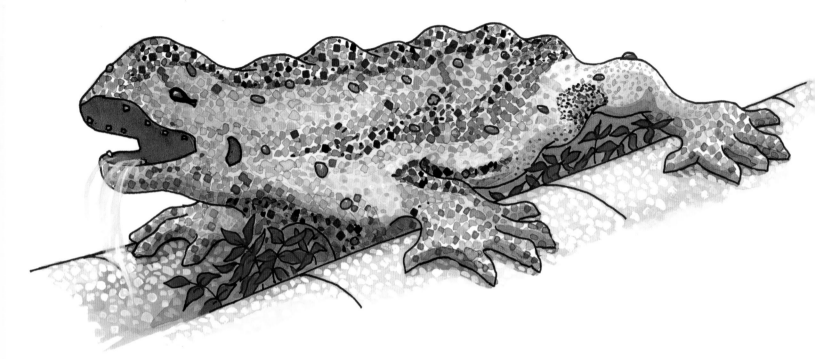

guarding the "Hall of the Hundred Columns." As for the buildings inside, one has a roof shaped like a mushroom; another is topped with upturned coffee cups. Obviously, Gaudí felt free to be his own outrageous self. One large open space (now often used as a children's soccer field) is bounded by an incredibly long, snaking ceramic bench. Looking for a particular kind of warped surface for it, a plaster mold that could be used repeatedly, Gaudí asked one of his workers to take his trousers off and sit on a bed of wet plaster.

Casa Milá, a six-story apartment building on the same avenue as Casa Batlló, looks rather like a man-made mountain. Pale and bulky, with a grotto-like entranceway, it soon became the butt of jokes and newspaper cartoons. Because of its soft, swelling shapes, some likened it to human lips, others to pastries, and one cartoonist depicted it as a hornet's nest. Still, despite criticism, many people loved it, not the least those who chose to live there.

Gaudí is often considered Spain's most prominent exponent of Art Nouveau (New Art), a style of decoration and architecture that flourished in the late nineteenth and early twentieth centuries. Art Nouveau typically involves flowers, leaves, and long undulating lines. These design elements are also characteristic of Gaudí. Yet his creations are too passionate, too wildly individualistic to be counted as a style other than his own.

Gaudí spent the last twenty years of his life working on Sagrada Familia, the Holy Family cathedral in Barcelona. It was an enormous undertaking. He wanted it to incorporate all his architectural knowledge, to be his life's work. He planned that the cathedral would have eighteen towers symbolizing the twelve apostles, the four evangelists, the Virgin Mary, and Christ, the last of which would be the tallest at 560 feet. Figures inside the cathedral were directly molded from nature. Gaudí found his models in the street, literally, and then photographed them from all angles. A textile merchant became King Solomon, a goatherd was chosen as Pontius Pilate. He even used a donkey to illustrate part of the flight into Egypt. A pelican, a web-footed sea tortoise, and a giant lizard are other creatures Gaudí used for his design. The Sagrada Familia—still unfinished—eventually became such an obsession with Gaudí that he set up residence in his on-site study, sleeping on a small cot.

As a young man, Gaudí had been extremely careful about the way he dressed. Something of a dandy, he would wear the finest leather gloves and sit in a carriage directing his workers. But that changed dramatically as he grew older and more involved with spirituality and strong Christian beliefs. He never married and increasingly became a recluse, unmindful of his appearance. In the end, this neglect may have contributed to his death.

On a spring evening in 1926, taking one last loving look at a Sagrada Familia tower that had just been completed, the seventy-four-year-old Gaudí, lost in a reverie, stepped off the sidewalk. Seconds later he was hit by a streetcar and knocked unconscious. Because of his wretched clothing—shoes with no socks and a worn-out jacket held together with safety pins—he was taken for a tramp and not immediately brought to a hospital. When someone finally recognized him, he was beyond help. He died three days later. Though few had ever met him or knew him by sight, Gaudí was a popular man. As he was taken to his final resting place at Sagrada Familia, more than half the city showed up, all dressed in mourning.

VAN ALEN & CHRYSLER

In early 1929, a race for the sky raged in New York City. People watched to see who would build the world's tallest building—the powerful Bank of Manhattan Trust Company down on Wall Street or Walter P. Chrysler, the automobile tycoon, up on 42nd Street? In late summer, the newspapers reported that the finished bank soared to an unprecedented 973 feet, just two irritating feet higher than had been planned for the Chrysler Building. To the "King of Cars," this was intolerable. Chagrined, Chrysler turned to his architect, William Van Alen, who decided to outfox the competition.

Five months later, New Yorkers looking up into the sky one November morning were treated to an extraordinary sight. Over a period of ninety minutes, a splendid tower, decorated with sunbursts of stainless steel and rows of triangular windows and topped by a thin silvery spire, emerged through the buildings's open roof. Van Alen had secretly assembled this shining crown in the building's fire shaft. Now, in one dramatic stroke, at 1,046 feet high (and 77 stories) soared the world's tallest building.

Van Alen had given Chrysler what he wanted: a structure that would "not merely scrape the sky but positively pierce it." Chrysler had also told his architect that it should declare the "glories of the modern age." Assuming that his boss was referring to the glories of his automobiles, Van Alen used details of cars as decorative elements. He modeled the spire on a radiator grille and went on to

install eight eagle-headed gargoyles, based on the hood ornament of a 1929 Chrysler Plymouth. Huge and silvery, they perch near the top of the building, looking as if they are about to take flight at any moment. Thirty-six stories above the street, there's a wraparound frieze of stylized cars with real metal hubcaps and, at each corner, four giant radiator caps. Surprisingly outfitted with wings, they also add to the notion that the whole building is poised for takeoff.

While the exterior of the Chrysler Building is bright and metallic, with a top that glistens in the sunlight, the lobby is dark and mysterious. Its walls are covered with sumptuous red Moroccan marble. On the ceiling, an elaborate mural called *Energy, Result, Workmanship and Transportation* depicts the building itself, along with construction workers, an airplane, and various decorative patterns. The elevator doors are particularly beautiful, with inlays of different rare woods and decorated with lotus buds—a concession to the Egyptomania that swept the world shortly after the discovery of the Tomb of Tutankhamen in 1923.

For a few glorious months, until the Empire State Building took over as the world's tallest structure (1,252 feet) in March of 1931, Chrysler relished his Number One status. He arranged to have an office suite and a lavish apartment near the top of the building, boasting to friends and foes alike that his was the highest toilet in the city. So there he sat, on his porcelain throne, delighting in his elevated position.

Chrysler and Van Alen expected rave reviews for the Chrysler Building when it was completed. It didn't happen. "The height of commercial swank," sneered *The New York Times*. "Stunt design, with no significance as serious design," sniffed *The New Yorker*. A third newspaper was even more disdainful, ridiculing the spire for having the "appearance of an uplifted swordfish."

To make things worse, the Chrysler Building was very much a product of the Jazz Age and the Roaring Twenties—an era of extravagance and elegance, which ended abruptly with the Stock Market crash in October 1929. From the start, this excessive skyscraper must have seemed a little out of place, a disagreeable reminder of a more reckless era. It was a great achievement but failed to be the unqualified success its architect had hoped for.

Born in Brooklyn in 1883, William Van Alen was famous for being somewhat of a maverick, a trendsetter who loved modernism and rejected the traditional. After graduating as an architect from the renowned Ecole des Beaux-Arts in Paris, where he was sent on a scholarship, he returned to New York in 1911. "No old stuff for me!" he is said to have exclaimed on his arrival. "No bestial copyings of arches and columns and cornices. Me, I'm new!" He worked for several firms in New York and, for some years, in partnership with H. Craig Severance—later his greatest rival as the architect in charge of the bank building down on Wall Street. The Chrysler Building was supposed to be Van Alen's crowning achievement. Instead, it began to look like a failure.

But things change. Now, over seventy years later, the Chrysler Building is many people's favorite skyscraper. Flush with zigzags, geometric patterns, and sleek streamlined forms, it is recognized as an outstanding example of Art Deco, the decorative style of the twenties and thirties. Critics hail the gargoyles as "poetry in steel" and trumpet the elevator doors as masterpieces of design. Above all, there's the incomparable swordfish-nose spire.

One of Van Alen's aims had been to have the triangular windows illuminated at night. They were, but not until the 1980s, many years after his death in 1954. As a result, every night the Chrysler Building now launches into the Manhattan sky with all the fantasy and glitter of the Jazz Age.

Van Alen surely would have liked that.

Bibliography

Filippo Brunelleschi 1377–1446

King, Ross. *Brunelleschi's Dome: How a Renaissance Genius Reinvented Architecture.* New York: Walker & Company, 2000.

Mimar Koca Sinan 1489–1588

Goodwin, Godfrey. *A History of Ottoman Architecture.* Baltimore: Johns Hopkins Press, 1971.

Antônio Francisco Lisboa 1738–1814

Bury, John B. "Estilo Aleijadinho and the Churches of Eighteenth-Century Brazil." *Architectural Review* 111 (February 1952): 92–100.

Mann, Graciela & Hans. *The Twelve Prophets of Aleijadinho.* Austin, Texas: University of Texas Press, 1967.

Smith, Robert C., Jr. "The Colonial Architecture of Minas Gerais in Brazil." *Art Bulletin* 21 (June 1939): 110–159.

The Roeblings (John, 1806–1869; Washington, 1837–1926; Emily, 1843–1903)

Mann, Elisabeth. *The Brooklyn Bridge: A Wonders of the World Book.* New York: Mikaya Press, 1996.

McCullough, David. *The Great Bridge: The Epic Story of the Building of the Brooklyn Bridge.* New York: Simon & Schuster, 1972.

Trachtenberg, Alan. *Brooklyn Bridge: Fact and Symbol.* Chicago: The University of Chicago Press, 1979.

Alexandre-Gustave Eiffel 1832–1923

Barthes, Roland. *The Eiffel Tower and Other Mythologies.* Translated by Richard Howard. New York: Hill and Wang, 1979.

Harriss, Joseph. *The Tallest Tower: Eiffel and the Belle Epoque.* Boston: Houghton Mifflin, 1975.

Antoni Gaudí 1852–1926

Carmel-Arthur, Judith. *Antoni Gaudí: Visionary Architect of the Sacred and the Profane.* London: Carlton Books Limited, 1999.

Collins, George R. *Antoni Gaudí.* New York: George Braziller, Inc., 1960.

Mower, David. *Gaudí.* London: Oresko Books Ltd., 1977.

Van Hensbergen, Gijs. *Gaudí.* New York: HarperCollins, 2001.

William Van Alen 1883–1954

Stravitz, David. *The Chrysler Building: Creating a New York Icon, Day by Day.* New York: Princeton Architectural Press, 2002.

OTHER BOOKS

Bagenal, Philip & Jonathan Meades. *The Illustrated Atlas of the World's Great Buildings: A History of World Architecture from the Classical Perfection of the Parthenon to the Breathtaking Grandeur of the Skyscraper.* London: Salamander Books Ltd., 1980.

Crosbie, Michael J. & Steve, and Kit Rosenthal. *Arches to Zigzags: An Architecture ABC.* New York: Harry N. Abrams, 2000.

Greenberg, Jan, and Sandra Jordan. *Frank O. Gehry: Outside In.* New York: Harry N. Abrams, 2000.

Isaacson, Philip M. *Round Buildings, Square Buildings & Buildings That Wiggle Like a Fish.* New York: Alfred A. Knopf, 1988.

Macaulay, David. *Building Big.* Boston: Houghton Mifflin / Walter Lorraine Books, 2000.

————. *Mosque.* Boston: Houghton Mifflin / Walter Lorraine Books, 2003.

Maddex, Diane. *Architects Make Zigzags: Looking at Architecture from A to Z.* New Jersey: John Wiley & Sons, 1986.

Newhouse, Elisabeth L., editor. *The Builders: Marvels of Engineering.* Washington, D.C.: National Geographic Society, 1992.

Rybczynski, Witold. *The Look of Architecture.* New York: Oxford University Press, 2001.

The World Atlas of Architecture (English edition of *Le Grand Atlas de l'Architecture Mondiale*). New York: Portland House, 1988.